T0197466

Rebirth

of a *Garden*

Daniel Pizzo

AuthorHouse™
1663 Liberty Drive
Bloomington, IN 47403
www.authorhouse.com
Phone: 1 (833) 262-8899

Because of the dynamic nature of the Internet, any web addresses or links contained in this book may have changed since publication and may no longer be valid. The views expressed in this work are solely those of the author and do not necessarily reflect the views of the publisher, and the publisher hereby disclaims any responsibility for them.

Any people depicted in stock imagery provided by Getty Images are models, and such images are being used for illustrative purposes only.
Certain stock imagery © Getty Images.

This book is printed on acid-free paper.

ISBN: 978-1-7283-7236-5 (sc)
ISBN: 978-1-7283-7263-1 (e)

Print information available on the last page.

Published by AuthorHouse   09/02/2020

authorHOUSE®

Rebirth

of a Garden

Your body is a garden.

My body is a garden.

Both of our gardens are beautiful.
But they are not the same.

Your garden has many amazing flowers. It is visited by unique bugs, has different leaves and weeds, and the dirt is your very own. The bugs, leaves, weeds, and dirt all effect how your garden blooms.

Both of our gardens grow at our own speed. We grow as our body wants, in our own unique ways.

Your flowers grow wild, and large, and bright. But sometimes, they do not.

My flowers grow wild, and large, and bright too! And sometimes, not.

Both of our gardens have visitors. Ants. Bees. Water. Sunshine. Wind and other visitors.

Sometimes, the bugs and the sunshine bring our gardens vitamins, which can help them grow stronger, with large flowers. Sometimes, our gardens have guests we don't want. These guests do not let our flowers grow pretty. The guests can be bugs that eat our flowers, or dirt which does not help our gardens grow. We are lucky though, because we have gardener doctors that help when there are too many unwanted guests.

We all have different types of weeds in our gardens. The weeds in our gardens often grow wild, large and are bigger than the flowers at times. When this happens, our bodies make sure to get rid of the weeds.

After our bodies rid the weeds, our flowers once again are the brightest in the box.

Today, I felt a weed growing in my garden. This was unlike the other growing weeds that we all have. My garden could not remove this weed. This weed was not brought by a guest germ. I asked my gardener doctor to check out this new weed. It was a strong, angry weed.

My gardener doctor could not pull this weed either!
The doctor clipped a part of the weed, to test and see
what it was.

His test – which he called a biopsy - said that this was a very different type of weed. A weed that not many gardens have.

My doctor used his microscope tool to look at this angry weed, to study this angry weed – and to figure out why it was so hard to pull. He told me he knew what this weed was. It is a cancer weed that is growing.

My body needs to pull the cancer weed. But it needs help to do so.

I am lucky, because my doctor gardener, knows other gardeners who also works with angry cancer weeds. We call them Oncology gardeners. There are a lot of doctor gardeners that know about these angry cancer weeds. The oncology gardeners will give my body help to pull the weeds. The help is what we call chemotherapy, which is short for Chemical Therapy. Chemotherapy uses medicines to remove the unwanted cancer weeds from someone's body.

Some oncology gardeners also work with Radiation gardeners. Radiation is a strong energy that the doctor gardeners zap the weeds with. The oncology and radiation gardeners are a great team!

With chemo and radiation help, my body will pull and zap all of the angry cancer weeds. There is one tough thing about the chemo and radiation help. The chemo help doesn't know the difference between angry cancer weeds, okay weeds, pretty flowers, or tall flowers. So, the chemo help must pull many weeds and flowers to get rid of the cancer weeds. And sometimes, the radiation energy zaps more than just the angry cancer weeds.

The chemo and radiation help make my garden feel extra dirty. Not beautiful. Not strong. But it must happen to stop the cancer weed from growing too large. The chemotherapy and radiation are working on my cancer weeds, are making them go away, but also, make other parts of my garden feel sick.

Once the cancer weeds are gone, once the radiation help works, my flowers will re-grow.

For my body, I am waiting for my cancer weeds to be gone. Waiting for my flowers to start to grow again.

Some people who had the angry cancer weed cannot re-grow their flowers. Do not re-grow any flowers.

This time, my flowers are re-growing. They will be strong and beautiful again. My garden has been changed forever, and is growing new, strong flowers. Re-growing my flowers is hard work. Tiring work. But I am growing, and getting tall, pretty flowers again. My garden is changing, and this is something that is different, and good!

My garden is strong without the angry weeds. My flowers want to grow, are ready to grow. My body will help them.

Your garden is amazing and strong.

Your flowers are bright. Our gardens together, are glowing.

We are beautiful.

Printed in the United States
By Bookmasters